DO YOU REALLY WANT TO VISIT MERCURY?

BY THOMAS K. ADAMSON

ILLUSTRATED BY DANIELE FABBRI

amicus illustrated

Amicus Illustrated is published by Amicus
P.O. Box 1329, Mankato, MN 56002
www.amicuspublishing.us

Library of Congress Cataloging-in-Publication Data
Adamson, Thomas K., 1970–
Do you really want to visit Mercury? / by Thomas K.
Adamson ; illustrated by Daniele Fabbri. — 1st ed.
p. cm. — (Do you really want to visit—?)
Audience: K-3.
 Summary: "A child astronaut takes an imaginary trip to
Mercury, learns about the harsh conditions on the rocky
planet, and decides that Earth is a good home after all.
Includes solar system diagram, Mercury vs. Earth fact
chart, and glossary"—Provided by publisher.
Includes bibliographical references.
ISBN 978-1-60753-195-1 (library binding) —
ISBN 978-1-60753-401-3 (ebook)
1. Mercury (Planet)—Juvenile literature. 2. Mercury
(Planet)—Exploration—Juvenile literature. I. Fabbri, Daniele,
1978– ill. II. Title. III. Series: Do you really want to visit—?
 QB611.A328 2014
 523.41—dc23   2012025969

Editor: Rebecca Glaser
Designer: The Design Lab

Printed in the United States of America at
Corporate Graphics in North Mankato, Minnesota.

Date 1/2013   PO 1145

9 8 7 6 5 4 3 2 1

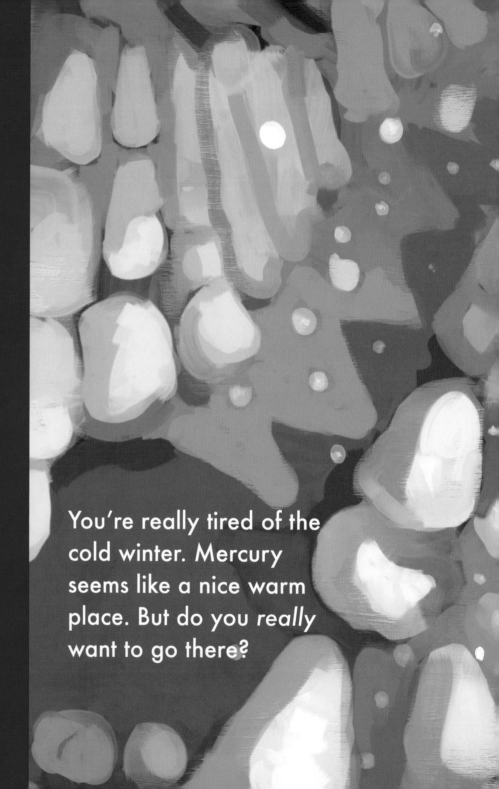

You're really tired of the cold winter. Mercury seems like a nice warm place. But do you *really* want to go there?

You'll need a spaceship that can travel nearly 50 million miles (80 million km)—and back. Even if you had a really fast spaceship, it would take two months to get there.

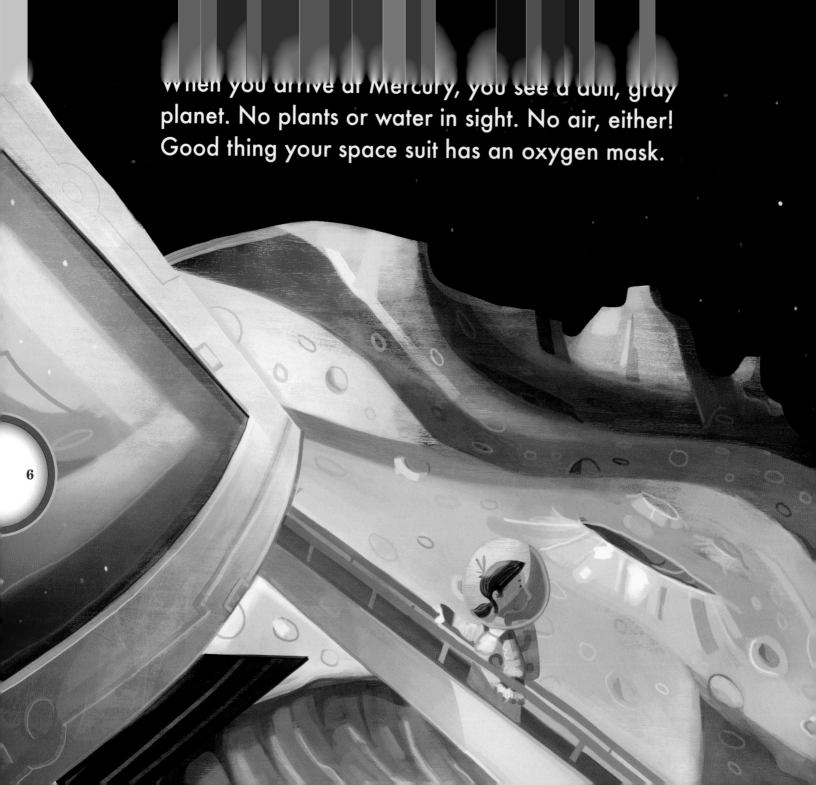

When you arrive at Mercury, you see a dull, gray planet. No plants or water in sight. No air, either! Good thing your space suit has an oxygen mask.

6

Mercury is very hot—and very cold! It's so close to the Sun that the daytime temperature makes your pizza oven feel cool.

At night, it's colder than the worst cold snap on Antarctica. Your space suit will have to protect you from these extremes. And it will be really dark at night—Mercury has no moon.

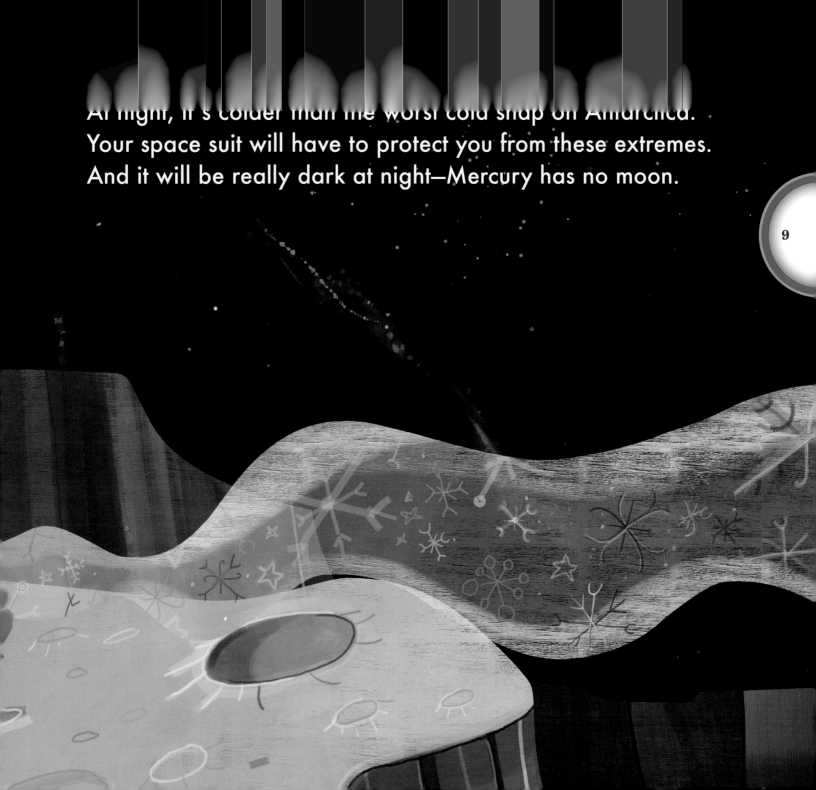

And nighttime will last a while. A Mercury day lasts as long as 176 days on Earth. Imagine eating lunch 176 times a day!

TODAY'S MENU
CHICKEN PATTY

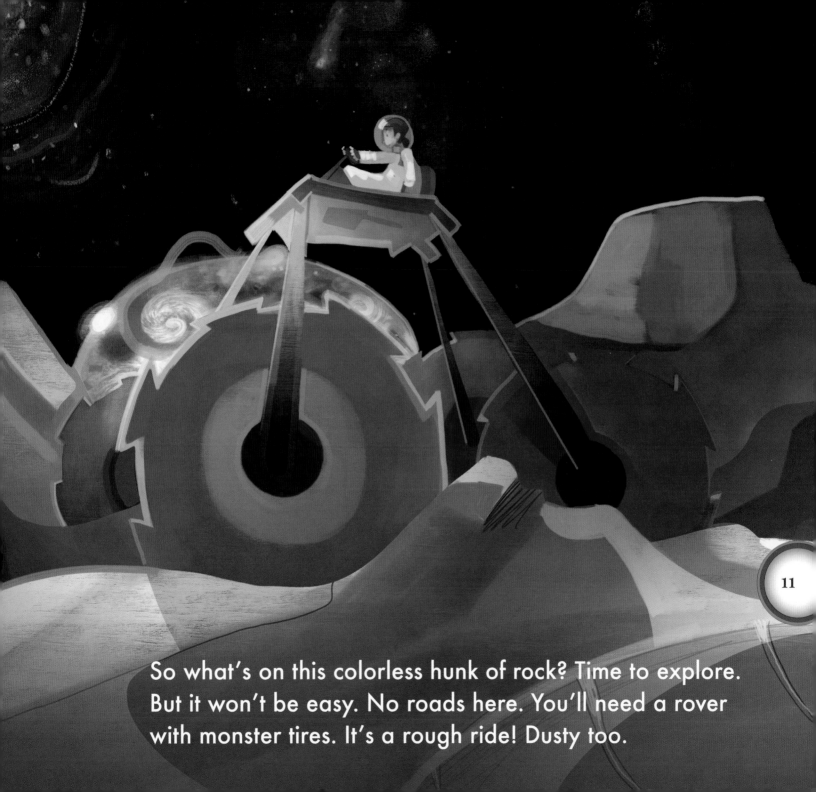

So what's on this colorless hunk of rock? Time to explore. But it won't be easy. No roads here. You'll need a rover with monster tires. It's a rough ride! Dusty too.

Ka-chunk! You've hit
your first crater.

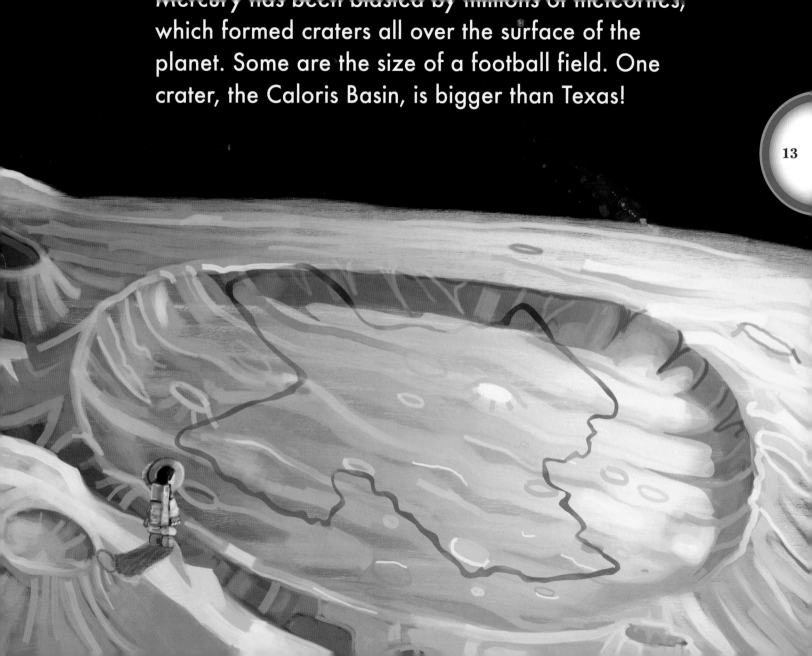

Mercury has been blasted by millions of meteorites, which formed craters all over the surface of the planet. Some are the size of a football field. One crater, the Caloris Basin, is bigger than Texas!

The Sun looks big here, since you're so close to it. Even with your heatproof space suit, you're getting thirsty. Wouldn't an ice cold drink be nice?

Mercury might seem like the last place in the solar system you'd find ice. But drive your rover to the poles. The craters here are always in shadow, so they're really cold all the time. Scientists think there may be some water ice sitting in those craters.

On the way back to the spaceship, check out Mercury's stunning rounded cliffs, called scarps. These rounded hills are like huge wrinkles in the planet's surface.

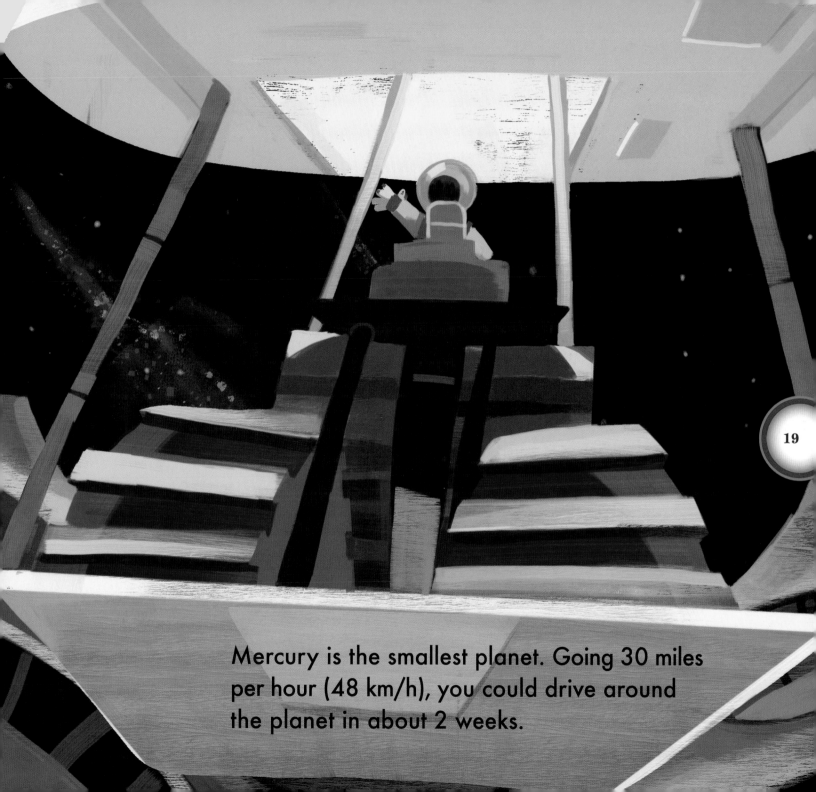

Mercury is the smallest planet. Going 30 miles per hour (48 km/h), you could drive around the planet in about 2 weeks.

Time to head home. It's much more comfy there—
warm but not too warm. Mercury is fun to explore,
but you *really* wouldn't want to live there.

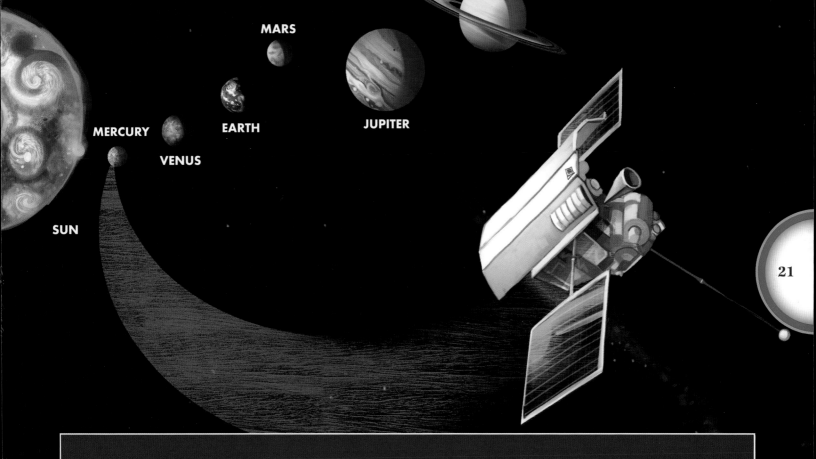

SUN

MERCURY

VENUS

EARTH

MARS

JUPITER

How Do We Know About Mercury?

We can't actually go to Mercury. So how do we know about this planet? Two unmanned spacecraft have explored Mercury. *Mariner 10* flew by Mercury in 1974 and 1975. It took pictures of less than half of the planet. *MESSENGER* began orbiting Mercury in March 2011. It sent back the best pictures yet of the surface, including the half no one had ever seen before.

Earth vs. Mercury

	Earth	Mercury
Position in solar system	Third from Sun	Closest to Sun
Average distance from Sun	93 million miles (150 million km)	36 million miles (58 million km)
Year (time to orbit Sun)	365 days	88 days
Day (sunrise to sunrise)	24 hours	176 days
Diameter	7,926 miles (12, 756 km)	3,032 miles (4,879 km)
Mass	1	About 18 Mercurys would equal the mass of Earth
Air	Oxygen and nitrogen	None
Water	About 70% covered with water	Possible ice in polar craters
Moons	1	0
Weather reporters	At least one in every major city	No need—Mercury has no weather.

Glossary

Antarctica The continent that covers Earth's South Pole; it has some of the coldest temperatures on Earth.

crater A large hole in the ground caused by a piece of rock from space hitting a planet or moon.

erode To wear away from rain or wind.

meteorite A piece of rock or metal from space that hits a planet or moon.

moon A body that circles around a planet.

oxygen A colorless gas that humans and animals need to breathe and is essential to life.

planet A large body that revolves around a sun.

rover A vehicle for exploring the surface of a planet or moon.

scarp A low, rounded cliff.

temperature How hot or cold something is.

Read More

Aguilar, David A. *11 Planets: A New View of the Solar System*. National Geographic, 2008.

Carson, Mary Kay. *Far-out Guide to Mercury*. Far-out Guide to the Solar System. Enslow, 2011.

Grego, Peter. *Voyage through Space*. QEB Space Guides. QEB Publishing, 2007.

James, Lincoln. *Mercury: The Iron Planet*. Our Solar System. Gareth Stevens, 2011.

Mist, Rosalind. *Mercury and Venus*. Up in Space. QEB Publishing, 2013.

Websites

MESSENGER Education: Fast Facts about Mercury
http://www.messenger-education.org/elusive_planet/fastfacts_index.php
View this site for animated diagrams that show what things look like on Mercury.

NASA Kids' Club
http://www.nasa.gov/audience/forkids/kidsclub/flash/
NASA Kids' Club features games, pictures, and information about astronauts and space travel.

NASA—MESSENGER—Unlocking the Secrets of Mercury
http://www.nasa.gov/mission_pages/messenger/main/index.html
View photographs of Mercury taken by the MESSENGER space probe and get the latest news.

About the Author
Thomas K. Adamson lives in Sioux Falls, SD, with his wife, two sons, and a dog. He has written dozens of nonfiction books for kids, many of them about planets and space. He enjoys sports, card games, reading with his sons, and pointing things out to them in the night sky.

About the Illustrator
Daniele Fabbri was born in Ravenna, Italy, in 1978. He graduated from Istituto Europeo di Design in Milan, Italy, and started his career as a cartoon animator, storyboarder, and background designer for animated series. He has worked as a freelance illustrator since 2003, collaborating with international publishers and advertising agencies.